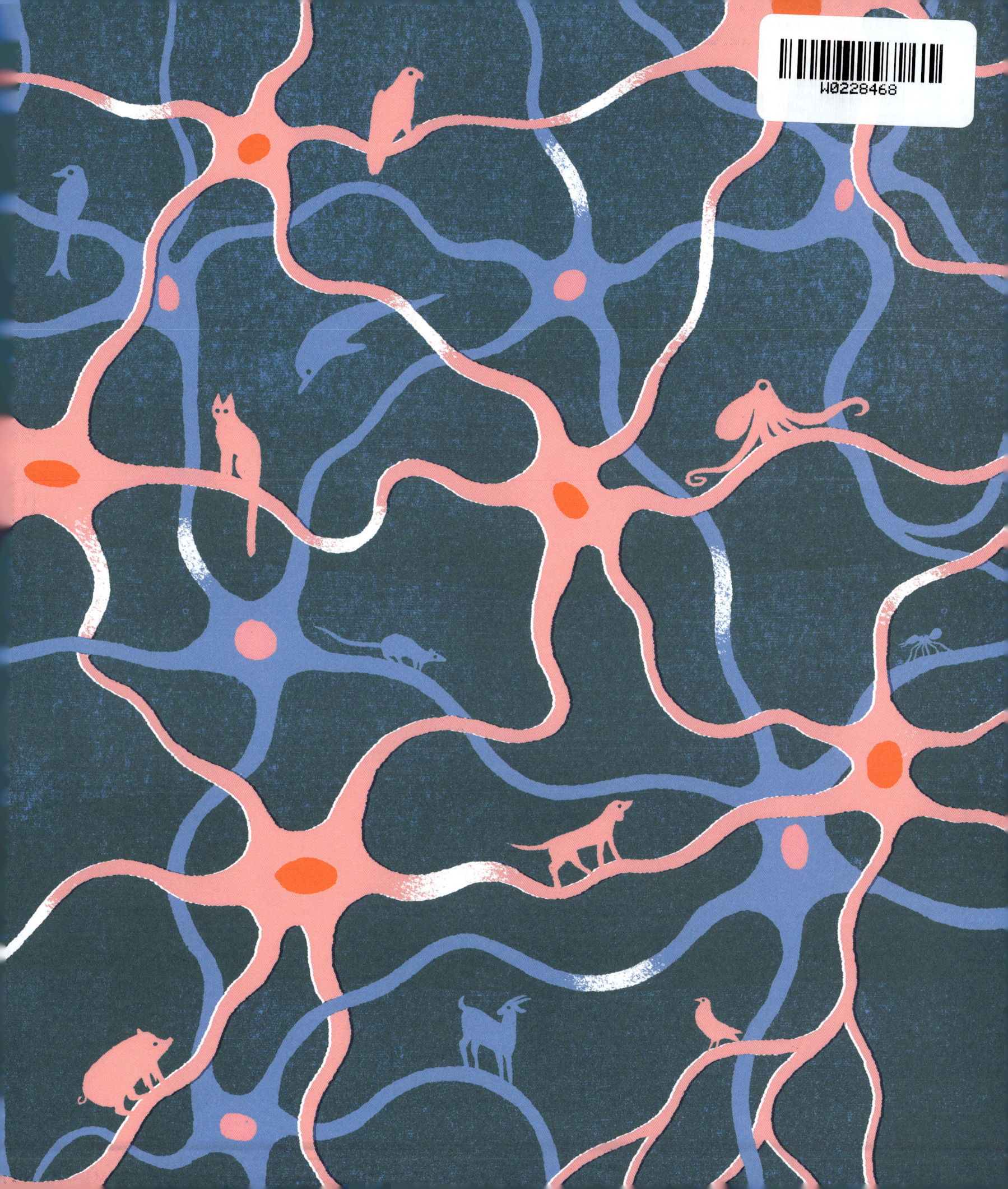

Smart Animals
Clever Creatures in the Animal Kingdom

Illustrated by Daniela Olejníková
Written by Michael Holland

This book was conceived, edited, and designed by Little Gestalten.

Edited by Robert Klanten and Fay Evans

Layout by Melanie Ullrich and Stefan Morgner

Typeface: Gabriel Sans by Svetoslav Simov

Printed by Schleunungdruck GmbH, Marktheidenfeld
Made in Germany

Published by Little Gestalten, Berlin, 2023
ISBN 978-3-96704-723-3

For more information, and to order books, please visit: www.little.gestalten.com

Bibliographic information published by the Deutsche Nationalbibliothek.
The Deutsche Nationalbibliothek lists this publication in the Deutsche
Nationalbibliografie; detailed bibliographic data are available online at www.dnb.de.

This book was printed on paper certified according to the standards of the FSC®.

Smart
ANIMALS

Clever Creatures in the Animal Kingdom

Written by Michael Holland
Illustrated by Daniela Olejníková

LITTLE
GESTALTEN

Contents

Introduction

You're a smart animal! The fact that you are holding this book and understanding the series of shapes on this page means that you have learned at least one language in your lifetime—pretty impressive when you come to think about it.

Human beings (*Homo sapiens*) are an incredible **species** and have managed to do so many amazing things in their 300,000 year history—controlling fire, domesticating plants and animals, creating, taming, and storing electricity, finding and using fossil fuels, creating languages, studying and understanding the world around us, building engines, glass, steel, computers, cars, submarines, rockets, bicycles, books, music, and so much more. We have also done some pretty bad things too—like polluting our planet and causing human suffering. But we are not the subject of this book!

The study of animal behavior is officially known as **ethology,** and although people have been observing animals for thousands of years (Roman scientist Pliny the Elder, who was born in AD 23 was an early example of an **ethologist**),

the modern science of **ethology** began in 1930s with the work of Dutch biologist Nikolaas Tinbergen, and Austrian biologists Konrad Lorenz and Karl von Frisch. When you watch a pet at home, or a bird in the park, you are being an **ethologist** too!

This book will zoom into the lives of some of the thousands of smart animals in the world–all able to use their amazing tool kits (their brains, bodies, senses, and instincts) in learning and remembering, being kind and caring, working and playing together, sharing, and problem solving.

To us, solving problems and puzzles is a fun way to exercise our brains, but to wild animals (and many people around the world), successful problem solving could be the difference between life and death. In the wild, the largest error of all is being eaten by someone else (a predator) or dying of thirst or starvation. All life on Earth is the result of things surviving to reproduce and pass down their genes to their young, and in some cases teaching them survival skills, too.

Is Intelligence the Same as Being Smart?

We compare many things in our lives—the prices of different items in a shop to get the best deal, the beauty of art to decide what movies, pictures, songs, poems or books are our favorites. We compare the speed of athletes to find the world champions, and in the natural world, we can compare lifespans, speed, height, weight, and brain size. This gives us a rough idea of intelligence, but what exactly is intelligence?

Well, according to one dictionary, "intelligence is the ability to acquire and apply knowledge and skills," and it's generally thought that the larger the brain an animal has, the more intelligent it is. So, using this rule, a frog is less intelligent than a cat. Perhaps that's true, but what about comparing two cats with the same brain size? We might find that they actually differ in their intelligence, just like people do.

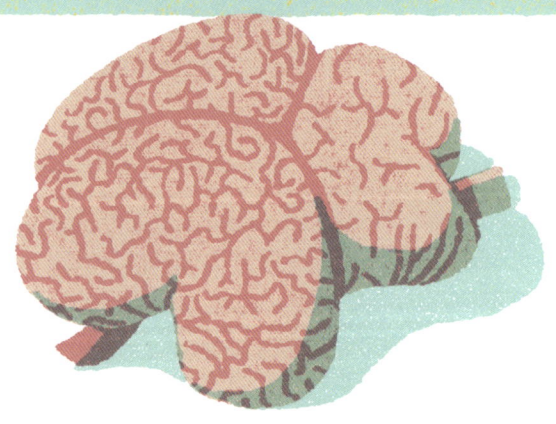

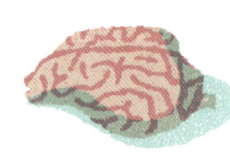

Amongst mammals, humans have a relatively large brain to body size and we have managed to do a lot with our brains—in fact, we're an amazing **species**! The sperm whale has a brain weighing up to 20 lbs (9 kg), but since its body can weigh 88 tons (80 tonnes), it has a lower relative brain to body size than us . . . but does that make it less intelligent?

Scientists have come up with something called the "encephalization quotient" (EQ), which is a measure of the relative size of the brain of a particular **species** compared with the expected value for members of the group to which it belongs. So, modern humans have an EQ of roughly six, meaning that our brain weight is six times more than a typical mammal. This is used as a rough guide to intelligence.

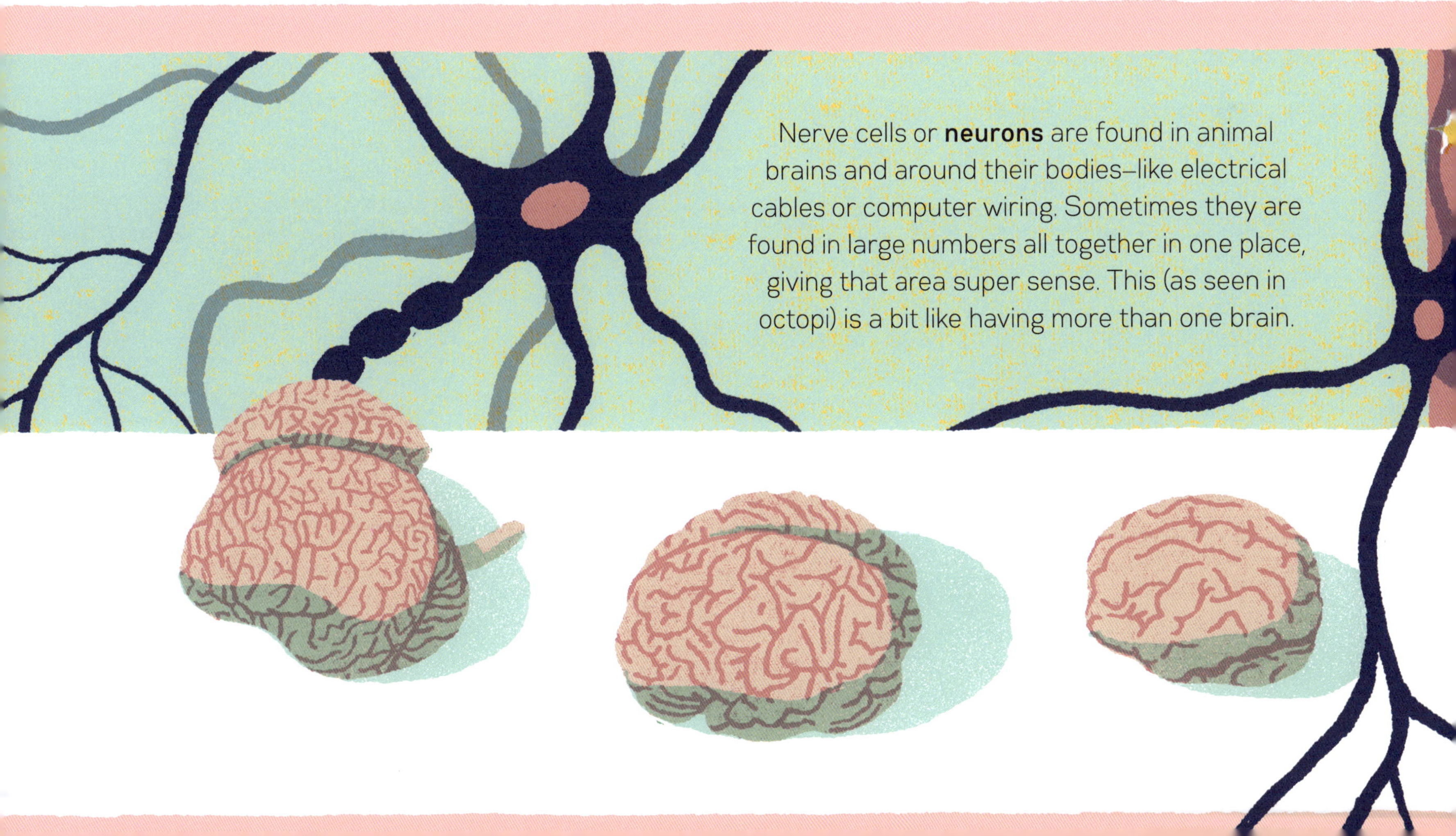

Nerve cells or **neurons** are found in animal brains and around their bodies—like electrical cables or computer wiring. Sometimes they are found in large numbers all together in one place, giving that area super sense. This (as seen in octopi) is a bit like having more than one brain.

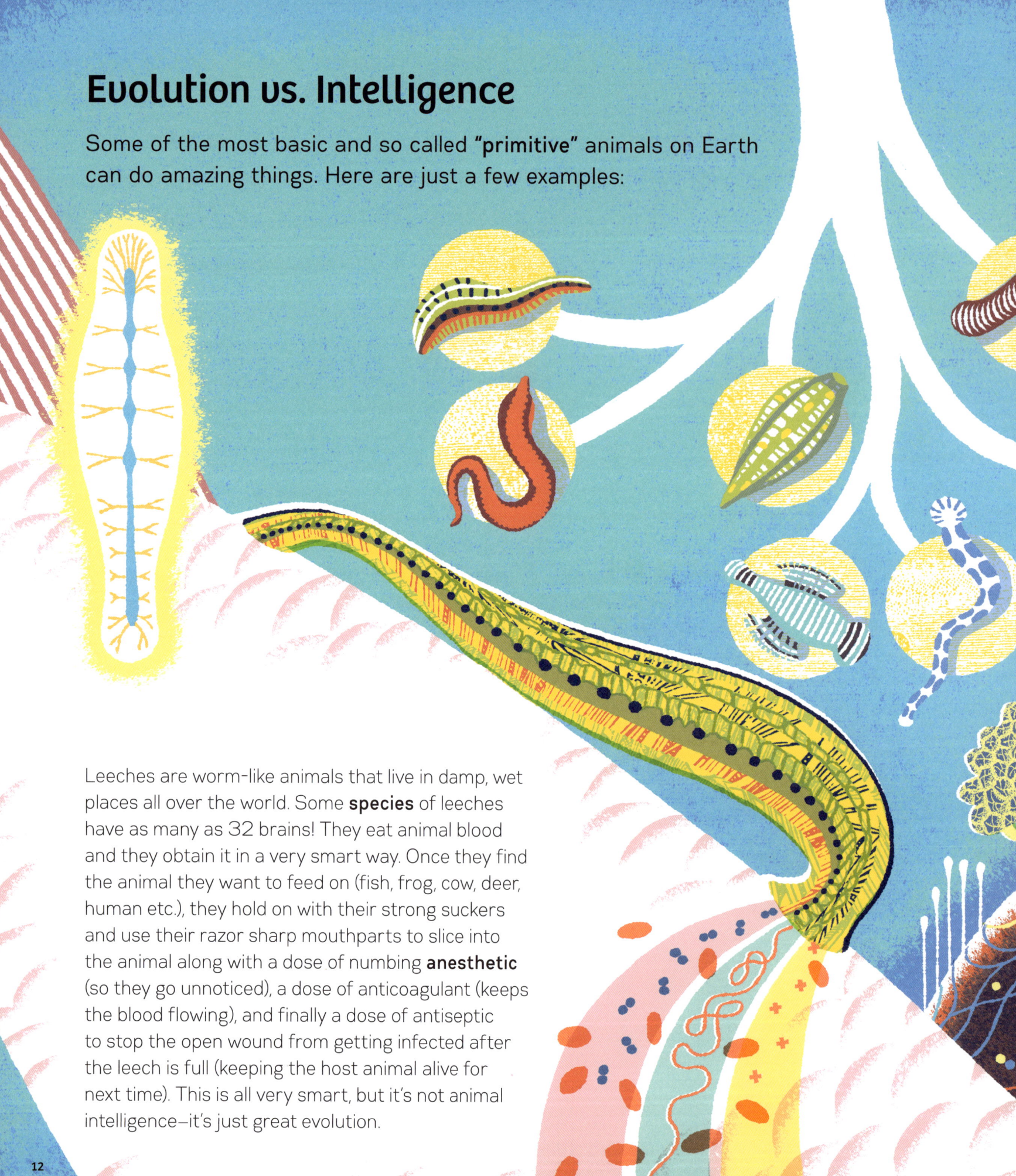

Evolution vs. Intelligence

Some of the most basic and so called **"primitive"** animals on Earth can do amazing things. Here are just a few examples:

Leeches are worm-like animals that live in damp, wet places all over the world. Some **species** of leeches have as many as 32 brains! They eat animal blood and they obtain it in a very smart way. Once they find the animal they want to feed on (fish, frog, cow, deer, human etc.), they hold on with their strong suckers and use their razor sharp mouthparts to slice into the animal along with a dose of numbing **anesthetic** (so they go unnoticed), a dose of anticoagulant (keeps the blood flowing), and finally a dose of antiseptic to stop the open wound from getting infected after the leech is full (keeping the host animal alive for next time). This is all very smart, but it's not animal intelligence—it's just great evolution.

Another really brilliant bit of evolution is found in jellyfish who have been around for around 500 million years so far. There is at least one tiny **species** (Turritopsis dohrnii) that can revert back to its larval form before becoming an adult again (like a butterfly changing back into a caterpillar before becoming a butterfly again). This animal, along with other jellyfish doesn't have a brain, but it's pretty clever to be able to live forever!

Right beneath your feet is an unseen world. It's the kingdom of fungi, including molds, mildews, and mushrooms. Until the middle of the 20th Century they were part of the Plant Kingdom, but scientists (called Taxonomists) realized that they deserved to be in a Kingdom of their own. Because they engulf their food and digest it, they are actually closer to animals than they are to plants. Some can spread for many miles, unseen. Others can get into ants' brains and control their minds! In the forests of the world the multi-branching roots of fungi act like network cables carrying nutrients between tree roots—this has been called the "Wood Wide Web." So although not animals, fungi are certainly intelligent in many ways and essential to our existence.

Raccoon

With their facial markings they already look like mischievous, masked bandits, and they live up to their looks. Raccoons are troublesome and persistent when they live in towns and cities where human food and rubbish is plentiful—even getting into houses to find food.

Raccoons (*Procyon lotor*) are nocturnal, **omnivorous** mammals and in the wild, feed on worms, insects, eggs, shellfish, frogs, small mammals, fruits, and nuts. They live in forests and woods near fresh water and are native to North America, but they are **naturalized** in many other parts of the world. A raccoon's eyesight isn't great, but they make up for this with their senses of smell, hearing, and touch.

WANTED

In North America they used to be hunted and killed by the thousands for their soft and warm fur to make hats—fancy that!

They have excellent memories and although they don't have **opposable thumbs,** this doesn't stop them being **dextrous** and able to cause trouble by opening locks, trashcans, and doors in urban areas where they have earned their status as a "pest" in their successful searches for food.

In laboratory studies, raccoons learned how to use a coin to operate a vending machine to get food. They have also been seen to remember solutions to things years later—so with nimble hands, great senses (mostly), and the ability to learn and remember, raccoons certainly earn their place in the smart charts!

Squirrel

There are around 300 **species** of squirrel in the world, made up of three main types of rodent: Ground, Flying, and Tree squirrels.

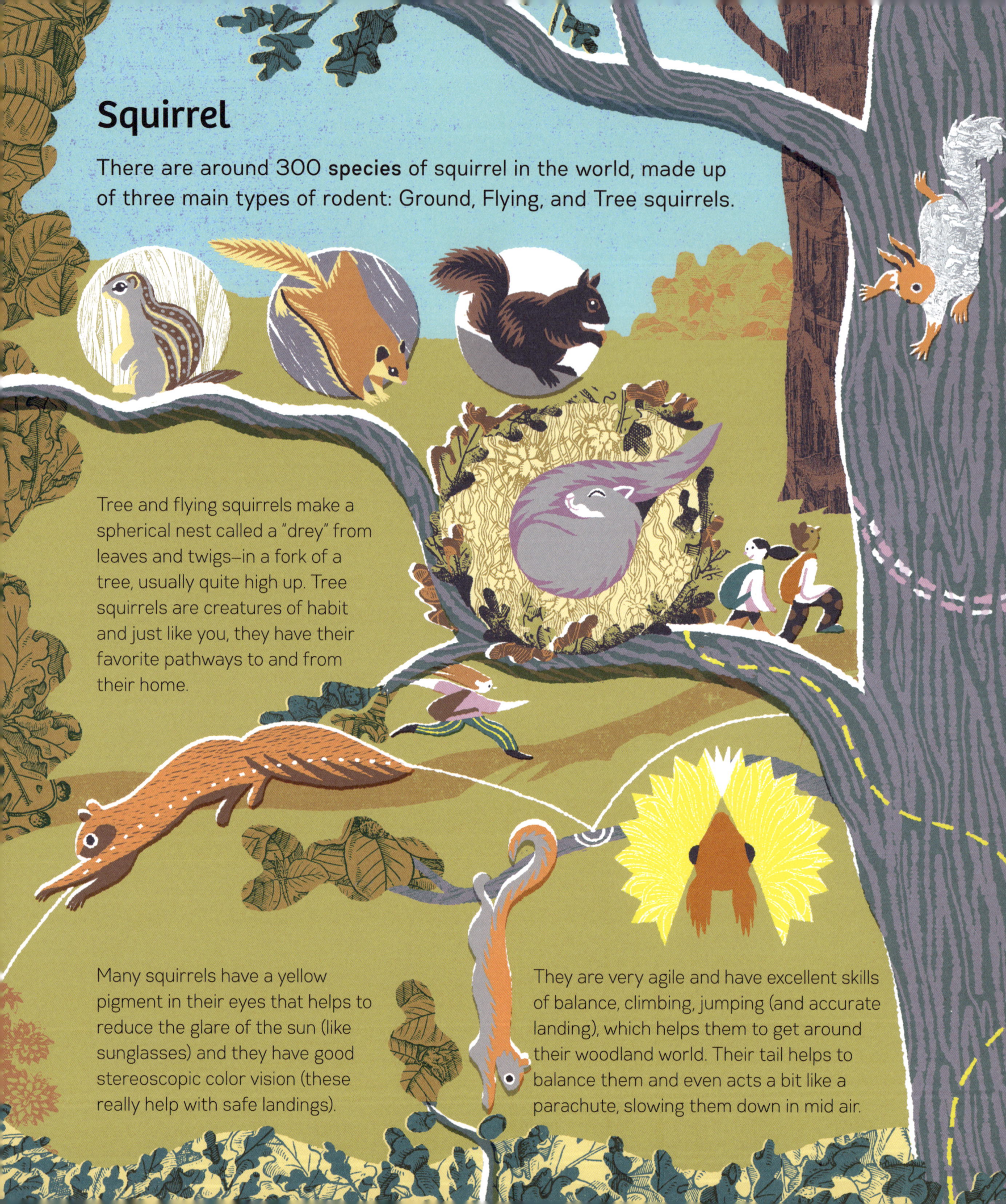

Tree and flying squirrels make a spherical nest called a "drey" from leaves and twigs—in a fork of a tree, usually quite high up. Tree squirrels are creatures of habit and just like you, they have their favorite pathways to and from their home.

Many squirrels have a yellow pigment in their eyes that helps to reduce the glare of the sun (like sunglasses) and they have good stereoscopic color vision (these really help with safe landings).

They are very agile and have excellent skills of balance, climbing, jumping (and accurate landing), which helps them to get around their woodland world. Their tail helps to balance them and even acts a bit like a parachute, slowing them down in mid air.

A crow relative called the Jay (*Garrulus glandarius*) has a similar diet to that of red and grey squirrels and also has the habit of burying seeds to save for later. Jays watch squirrels to see where they have buried their food and then steal it. Smart squirrels sometimes pretend to bury food underground to trick potential thieving jays . . .

In many places, squirrels have become a common part of the urban garden and can often be seen chewing through (sometimes upside down) and emptying bird feeders as well as digging up lovingly planted bulbs and seeds.

Some ground squirrels have been seen to chew rattlesnake skin before smearing them onto their bodies to mask their own squirrelly smell from potential predators—pretty smart, eh!?

They feed on seeds, nuts fruits, berries, fungi, eggs, and baby animals and often bury extra food in the ground to come back to later (using memory and smell to find their edible treasures). If a squirrel forgets where it buried a seed (such as an acorn), or perhaps is killed after doing this, the seed stands a good chance of going into an Oak tree, dispersed by the squirrel away from the parent tree.

Honey Bee

Worldwide, there are around 25,000 **species** of bees, but only eight **species** honey bees. They make honey as it's a great source and store of sugar, protein, and water.

Honey bees have incredibly organized societies, with clearly defined roles and responsibilities. The three types of honey bee in a **colony** are:

The Queen An egg laying machine who can lay 2000 eggs per day (and night—she doesn't stop). A Queen bee can live for around five years.

The Worker Bees These are all females (around 60,000 of them!) and go through a series of age-related jobs in their short 6 week life—feeding and caring for the Queen and the larvae, cleaning away and disposing of dead bee bodies, air conditioning (by flapping their wings), security guard (making sure that only bees from that colony enter), foraging for water, nectar and pollen, scouting for new places to start a new colony and looking for Drones for the Queen to mate with.

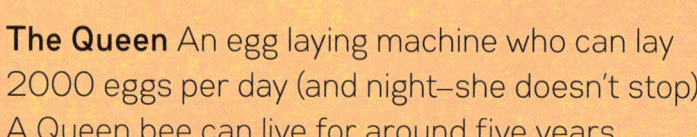

The Drones These are males and in a typical bee hive there are around 2000 of these. Their main job is to mate with the Queen if chosen (she only does this with around 15 in her life).

Apis mellifera is the **species** from which the majority of our honey comes from. Their wing muscles need temperatures of 10°C and above in order to work, so they can't fly under this temperature—which in many parts of the world can be most of the Autumn, all of the winter and some of the spring! So, collecting nectar, pollen, and water during the warmer months and converting it onto honey means that a colony of honey bees can survive long periods of cold weather.

If a **colony** is doing really well, the Queen might decide to create a new hive somewhere else, so she'll send her worker scouts out to look for suitable locations. This will also happen if the colony isn't doing well (due to a lack of food, water, or other threats).

These scouts present their findings via "dance offs" where they try to persuade the other worker bees that their location is better than others. Non-scout workers then go and visit these potential locations to see which is the most suitable.

This isn't the only type of dance they do—when returning from a food collecting trip (it takes a million journeys to make a jar of honey and a worker will make around a teaspoon of honey in her lifetime), a worker will perform a "waggle dance" to tell others where the source of the nectar was.

10 000 000

Scientists have tried using "fences" made of honey bee hives in Africa to deter elephants from entering farmland (that's more us being smart enough to try this, to be honest). It's thought that the buzzing deters the elephants.

Octopus

There are around 300 **species** of Octopus, but the Common octopus (*Octopus vulgaris*) seems to be the one most studied.

Certainly one the brainiest of all animals, octopi have nine of them (well, kind of)! As well as their main brain (found in their head), which is the and is the largest of all **invertebrate** brains, at the end of each of their eight arms there are clusters of cells called which act like mini brains (**neurons** are cells that make up an animal's nervous system–like cables carrying information). This allows octopus arms to be sensitive to touch and temperature, but also to detect changes in light, color, and taste. Imagine if you could do that with your arms!

Around 2000 years, ago a Roman naturalist and author Pliny the Elder observed an octopus wedging a small stone into the opening of a bivalve (creatures with two shells like clams, mussels, and oysters) so that it could more easily prise it open to eat it. This is a great example of tool use, which shows great intelligence. This phenomenon has also been recorded by modern day scientists.

Did you know:

In invertebrates, a "tentacle" has suckers just at its tip, but an "arm" has suckers along its whole length.

Another good example of these creatures using "tools" found nearby is when a captive octopus named Otto was seen picking up and throwing rocks from his aquarium to break lightbulbs above him because they were too bright!

In other experiments, octopi have been seen to unscrew the lids of jars, successfully navigating mazes, and when given the choice of either going into a "room" with a picture of a shark (predator) or a room with a picture of a crab (food) on the outside of it, they always went towards the food side. They can remember the location of food and they have been shown to learn by watching a video tutorial on how to open a box containing food. Before being shown the video, they couldn't work out how to open the box.

TU3E

Octopi also have the amazing abilities of changing color (to show their mood and for camouflaging themselves) and of being able to squeeze through very small spaces.

Ant

So far, around 12,500 **species** of ants have been discovered, but it's thought that there might be twice as many out there . . .

Leaf-cutter ants in many jungles of the world collect and carry pieces of leaves that they cut from plants as far away as 330 ft (100 meters) from their huge underground nests. This is the equivalent of you carrying something that weighs 600 lbs (270 kg)— like a grand piano—between your teeth, and running at high speed!

Inside these nests (that are like huge cities with 10 million residents), they carefully clean and cut the leaves into smaller pieces onto which they spread bits of mature fungus, and then add to the leaf pile—this fungus then grows and digests the leaves. Eventually the ants then feed the nutritious fungus to their larvae to help them to grow. Adult leaf-cutter ants feed on the sap of the leaves they are collecting.

Plants can sense that their leaves are being destroyed by these ants (who can strip a tree of all of its leaves in a few hours) and some (such as Bixa), start filling their leaves with toxins when they sense trouble. The ants carry on collecting the leaves, taking the toxins back to the fungus which gradually feels unwell and weakens. The fungus senses this too and "tells" the ants to change to a different plant **species** for the time being, so they do—they are following orders from a fungus!

Even though the ants have a highly organized society, these fungi are even smarter than the ants as they are actually working for it in a way, by keeping it alive and helping it to grow.

When the Amazon river's level rises, the forest floods. Colonies of Amazonian fire ants (Solenopsis spp) have been seen to "hold hands" to form rafts that float to the safety of a tree trunk which they can climb up.

Dolphin

There are 42 **species** of dolphins and they can be found almost all over the world. Perhaps the most recognisable is the Bottlenose dolphin (*Tursiops truncates*) which can live for around 50 years and can grow to around 13 ft (4 meters) long.

People started catching bottlenose dolphins to keep as early as the 1860s, but the first dolphin was not displayed in a public aquarium until 1947. This must have been quite a spectacle to see—these graceful and athletic ocean mammals are wonderful to watch up close. It's highly likely that keeping dolphins (that travel around 37 miles (60 km) per day in the wild) in captivity isn't particularly good for their minds and bodies, but on the other hand it does help us to understand them more and appreciate them. Today, there are many organizations dedicated to their conservation.

MARINE STUDIOS

With their powerful sense of hearing, it's been found that dolphins can recognize and remember the sounds of individual boats, using this to avoid hunters they'd seen before.

Dolphins have been found to have their own names for themselves which they use when talking to each other (in a combination of whistles, clicks, cracks, grunts, and squeaks). In a laboratory study of 1965, two bottlenose dolphins named Dash and Doris were kept in separate tanks but connected by an underwater phone. When they could hear each other, their sounds were coordinated into what looked and sounded like a conversation, but when the sound wasn't connected, they both spoke less and their sounds were much more random.

In scientific studies, bottlenose dolphins that had various shapes drawn onto them looked at themselves in an (underwater) mirror before moving their bodies into a position so they could see the shapes more clearly. To us, this might seem obvious, as we understand that the image in a mirror is us and not someone else, but many animals (and even human babies before they are 18 months old) simply can't comprehend this at all. The mirror test is certainly a sign of intelligence and self-awareness.

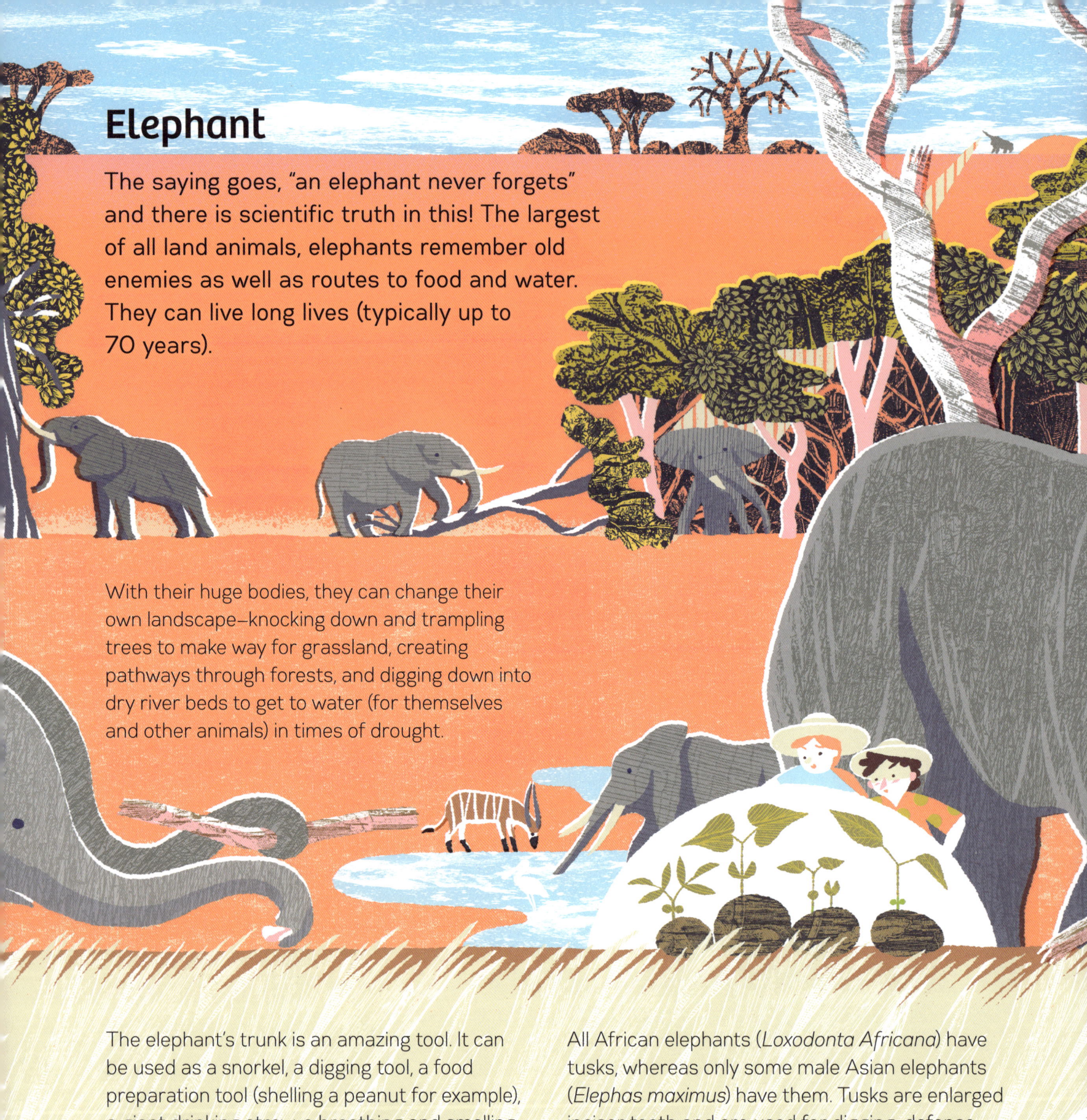

Elephant

The saying goes, "an elephant never forgets" and there is scientific truth in this! The largest of all land animals, elephants remember old enemies as well as routes to food and water. They can live long lives (typically up to 70 years).

With their huge bodies, they can change their own landscape—knocking down and trampling trees to make way for grassland, creating pathways through forests, and digging down into dry river beds to get to water (for themselves and other animals) in times of drought.

The elephant's trunk is an amazing tool. It can be used as a snorkel, a digging tool, a food preparation tool (shelling a peanut for example), a giant drinking straw, a breathing and smelling device (it is, after all, a nose), and it's used for cuddling, playing, and more.

All African elephants (*Loxodonta Africana*) have tusks, whereas only some male Asian elephants (*Elephas maximus*) have them. Tusks are enlarged incisor teeth and are used for digging, defense, lifting, foraging—so, along with the flexible trunk, are valuable tools.

Unfortunately, the substance tusks are made from is called ivory which has also been valued by humans to make many different things from billiard balls and white piano keys to jewelry and more. This means that elephants were killed just for their tusks!

Elephants spend a large amount of their days eating and can walk 50 miles (80 km) per day looking for it. All this eating creates around 220 lbs (100 kg) of dung each day! This is rich, nutritious organic matter which also contains seeds from far away—so elephants are important for seed dispersal too (helping plants to travel).

After the death of an elephant, family and "friends" have been observed covering the body with branches, soil, and leaves before standing over it for days, gently touching its body with their trunks. When elephants come across elephant bones on their travels, they stop, become quiet, and gently pick up the bones.

If all this wasn't amazing enough, captive elephants have been trained to paint really accurate and beautiful pictures.

Rat

To many people, rats are unpleasant. This could be due to their links to the spread of disease, or the fact they don't mind living in sewers surrounded by our "business"! However, they are pretty smart creatures. We know this as they've been observed and experimented on since the 1850s—advancing our medicine, understanding of nerves, and our understanding of animal behavior. Rats make up around 95% of all lab animals.

Rattus norvegicus domestica, or the Lab Rat, have been shown to be able to successfully solve quite tricky puzzles and memorize mazes with complex routes. They demonstrate spatial learning, memory, reasoning, and being able to reflect upon previous experiences. In one experiment, a puzzle with eight spokes going outwards from a central starting point had food at the end of each path and a rat visited them all (not in order), but didn't go down the same path more than once. Researchers made sure that the rats weren't able to use scent to mark where they had been to help them, so their success was all down to their ability to remember and learn.

Young wild rats learn from their parents which foods are good and also the quickest way of getting to certain foods—adult rats in the pine forests of Israel have found that biting off the scales of pinecones from the base upwards gives quicker access to the pine seeds beneath. The less energy you use to get the food, the better! Young rats that had watched their parents doing this were much quicker in doing this for themselves when faced with a pine cone of their own than ones who hadn't.

Did you know:

Scientists have even built small cars for rats to drive and steer towards their food in the laboratory and they're pretty good drivers too!

Crow

There are around 30 **species** of crow around the world and their cousins include jays, magpies, rooks, and more. These are all highly evolved, intelligent birds that are able to adapt to their surroundings, whether they are in living in towns and cities, or forests and woods.

The New caledonian crows (*Corvus monoduloides*) have been observed using stones to displace water to drink and using sticks (tools) to get at insects inside rotting trees. This type of tool use has been seen in other types of crows around the world and through history. In fact, in the famous fable by the ancient Greek storyteller Aesop (around 2500 years ago) a crow does exactly this—placing pebbles into a pitcher of water in order to make the level rise (through displacement) so it could drink.

Did you know:

Given complex puzzles, crows take very little time to understand the series of steps needed to get to the food reward. Other animals (such as a human child) given the same puzzle didn't even realize it was a puzzle and thought it was just a toy!

In an experiment, wild crows were caught by people wearing masks of human faces. The crows were then looked after and fed by the same people wearing different masks. After four months, these crows learned the difference between the threatening faces and caring ones. It was also discovered that these facial memories were found in the same part of the crows' brains as we use for the same sorts of memories and associations. This tells us that not only are crows clever like us, we are "wired" in a similar way.

Termite

Termites are one of the most resourceful organisms on the planet. They are highly organized with a social structure where they each know who they are and what to do . . . and they do a lot!

There are three types of termite in a colony: Workers, Soldiers, and the Queen. Just like other "social insects" (such as honey bees, ants, and wasps) the Queen termite is far too busy giving birth to thousands of eggs every day to go out and do anything. Luckily, she has thousands of workers to do the work of the colony. As the name suggests, the soldiers protect everyone in the colony, which can range from a few hundred to five million individuals.

Termites build mounds above and below ground. The tallest ever recorded was in The Republic of Congo at 42 ft (12.8 meters) tall, but they're usually around 3–10 ft (1–3 meters). If termites were as tall as humans, their tallest mounds would be 460 ft (1500 meters) high! Using a combination of soil, sand, poop, and saliva, these mounds contain their home, farms, food stores, and nurseries. Efficiently crafted tunnels transport them around the colony and to the outside world–all with excellent ventilation and air conditioning! There are no termite bedrooms, because they don't sleep– imagine how much you'd accomplish if you didn't need to sleep, especially if there were five million of you!

Termites cannot digest cellulose (the substance that plants are made from), so most of them have bacteria or protozoa in their guts that do this for them. This is an example of a **symbiotic** relationship.

Some termite **species** (just like leaf-cutter ants) farm fungus that they grow in their mounds. The fungus breaks down the plant material for the termites which they then eat.

Soldiers and the Queen are fed a nutrient rich liquid by the workers via a process called trophallaxis. This liquid also gives young termites the necessary bacteria for their guts to help them to digest cellulose. While they are feeding other termites these fluids, they will also groom each other.

They are "programmed" to do all of this through their excellent evolution—the colony as a whole is a very smart and hugely efficient machine, which "thinks" and acts like one huge organism.

Chicken

Domestic chickens (*Gallus gallus domesticus*) were first **domesticated** from junglefowl around 8000 years ago (probably somewhere in China) for their eggs and meat. They were then taken all over the world where they have remained a popular farm animal.

A female chicken teaches her young language skills even before they are born. By the time they are adults, chickens have over 30 alarm calls and the ability to communicate with each other using sounds and body language. All in all, a complex language system.

Despite their reputation for being unintelligent, chickens are far from it. They've had plenty of evolutionary time (roughly 5 million years) to perfect their survival skills. In their original native jungle homes they'd be a tasty meal (and a good source of protein) for all sorts of predators, so survival, staying alert and being smart was essential to them.

From as little as a few hours old, chickens can tell the difference between five different objects and can understand size, too—always going for the largest food items! They also understand the idea that if an object can't be seen, it still exists (which takes a human baby a year to understand).

Chickens have full color vision and a great memory, which helps them to be able recognize over 100 fellow chicken faces as well as different foods when they are foraging for seeds, fruits, plants, worms, and insects. Not only that, they have the ability to use the position of the sun to navigate.

Chicken society is made up of a complex "pecking order" that determines who is most important. This is all worked out very early on while they are chicks. When they are around food, chicks will peck at each other until the strongest ones end up getting more food. By the time the are adults, everybody knows where they fit in the social ranking of strongest to weakest—with the strongest chickens getting to eat and drink first (and the most) and getting the first choice of where to sleep. Because everyone knows their place, they are quite a peaceful bunch of birds.

Goat

Living on exposed, dry mountains where it's often hard to find food and water has given goats toughness and sharp minds. There are around 300 breeds of domesticated goat, kept for their milk, meat, fur, and skin. If you ever meet one, you'll see it has character and personality—signs of a smart animal.

Goats have a great appetite for food and are famous for not being particularly fussy eaters. Goat keepers have reported that their clothes, hair, and shoes have all been nibbled at!

In an experiment, Nigerian dwarf goats were given artificial symbols presented in a four-choice design. The symbols belonged to two categories: category I, black symbols with an open center (rewarded with food) and category II, the same symbols but filled black (unrewarded). The goats managed to get the hang of this quickly, showing well developed **cognitive abilities** and memory.

They've been seen to be aware of human gestures—preferring smiling people with friendly body language. Goats have even been observed to look at what a human is pointing at, which is something we might take for granted, but is a gesture even humans had to learn once.

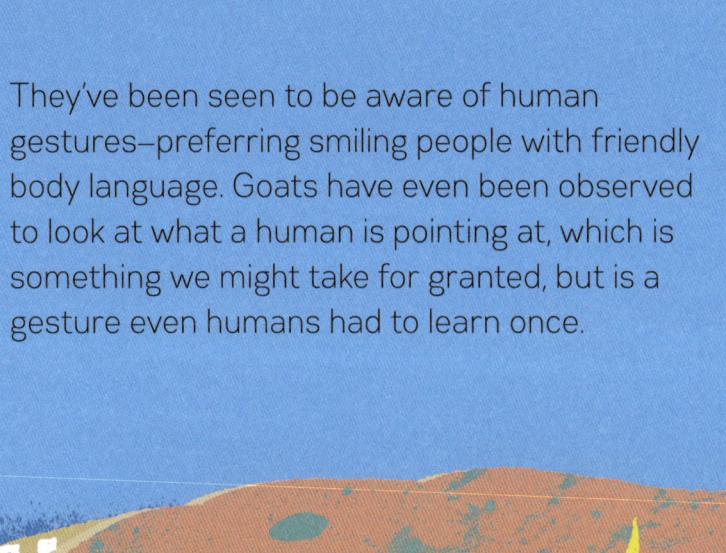

Goats tell each other apart by sound, smell, and by look and can remember things for a long time (they can live for around 17 years).

They are aware of emotions and can read the moods of other goats by sight and sound. Researchers suggest that a goat can be affected by the moods of those around it, just like us!

Did you know:

Scientists, wanting to make a large amount of spider silk for use in body armor and bullet-proof vests (as spider silk is light and very strong) inserted the spider silk gene into a goat and then tried to extract the silk from the goat's milk. It was successful, but cost too much to do.

Like all captive animals, domestic goats prefer to have things to do and to play with—mental and physical challenges to keep themselves happy and fit.

Squid

There are around 300 **species** of squid, with a huge amount of variety in the squid world. The smallest **species** measures just 0.7 in (18 mm) in length and the largest at over 42 ft (13 metres) long!

Along with a streamlined body, squid have two tentacles (with suckers at the end) and eight arms (with suckers all the way along) and, like octopi and cuttlefish, are molluscs (relatives of snails and slugs). They eat prawns, crabs, fish, shellfish, other (smaller) squid, and some sea plants like seaweed.

They use their two front tentacles to quickly grab their prey very precisely before cutting it up into smaller pieces with their beak. As well as using it to hide from their prey, some squid use their ability to change color to confuse and stun their prey, others inject them with poisonous saliva.

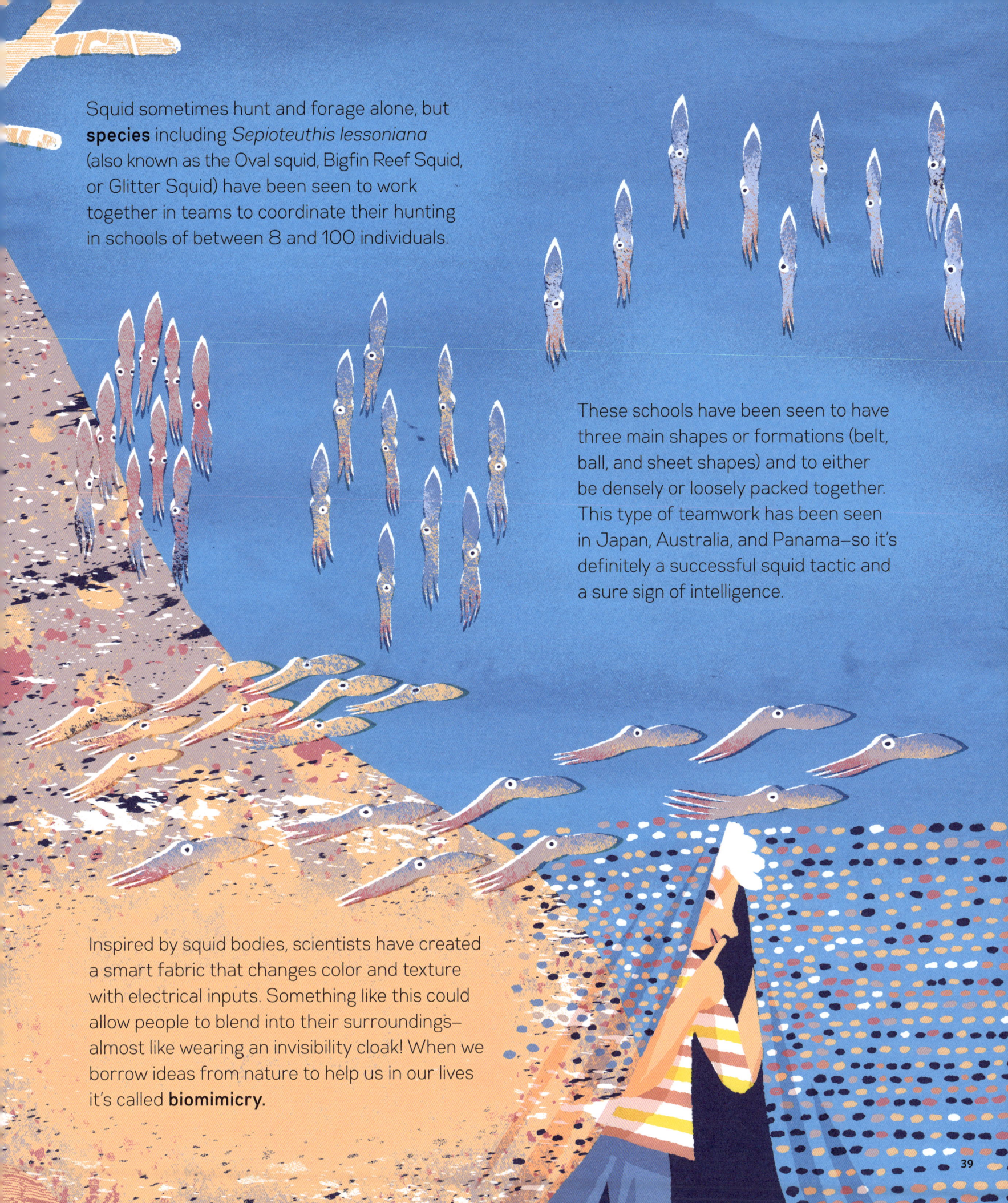

Squid sometimes hunt and forage alone, but **species** including *Sepioteuthis lessoniana* (also known as the Oval squid, Bigfin Reef Squid, or Glitter Squid) have been seen to work together in teams to coordinate their hunting in schools of between 8 and 100 individuals.

These schools have been seen to have three main shapes or formations (belt, ball, and sheet shapes) and to either be densely or loosely packed together. This type of teamwork has been seen in Japan, Australia, and Panama—so it's definitely a successful squid tactic and a sure sign of intelligence.

Inspired by squid bodies, scientists have created a smart fabric that changes color and texture with electrical inputs. Something like this could allow people to blend into their surroundings—almost like wearing an invisibility cloak! When we borrow ideas from nature to help us in our lives it's called **biomimicry**.

Pig

Pigs communicate with each other through body language, smell, and grunts, oinks, and squeals. These emotional animals are sensitive to what's going on around them.

Humans first **domesticated** wild boar around 8000 years ago, and nowadays there are hundreds of breeds of domestic pig in the world—mostly kept for their meat, though some are trained to find delicious and valuable underground fungi called truffles!

Remarkably, pigs have been taught how to play a basic computer game using a joystick with their snouts! Even after the reward (food) dispenser broke on the games machine, they carried on as the researchers praised and encouraged them with kind words. The researchers quoted former British Prime Minister, Winston Churchill by saying "Dogs look up to you, cats look down on you, and pigs look you right in the eye."

In laboratory experiments, two Vietnamese pot-bellied pigs (a breed of domestic pig) called Helga and Hamlet were not only able to recognize and learn what three different objects were called (frisbee, ball, dumbbell), but they also learned to understand and distinguish the words and gestures for these and for three actions (sit, fetch, jump).

When given verbal and physical combinations of the action and object symbols (e.g., "fetch the frisbee"), they managed to correctly perform the task presented to them. This is truly a remarkable example of animal intelligence and their ability to learn.

African Grey Parrot

One of the longest lived of all birds, African Grey parrots typically live for around 60 years in their forest habitat of central and East Africa, where their main foods are fruits, nuts, seeds, flowers, tree bark, snails, and insects. They are sociable animals, and a pandemonium of African grey parrots can contain around 100 birds (although they usually tend to forage with their life partner).

In the 1980s, a Grey Parrot called Alex was taught over 80 English words for colors, shapes, and materials and was able to successfully tell researchers when objects were similar (e.g. a red wooden triangle and a green rawhide triangle) or different (e.g., a red wooden square and a blue wooden square). This research was carried out by American ethologist and psychologist Irene Pepperberg. She wrote all about this in her book, "*Alex & Me: How a Scientist and a Parrot Discovered a Hidden World of Animal Intelligence—and Formed a Deep Bond in the Process.*"

In other research, German scientists (Désirée Brucks and Auguste von Bayern) decided to see if they have an altruistic (non-selfish) side. They found that African Grey Parrots voluntarily and spontaneously helped other parrots to achieve a goal, without obvious immediate benefit to themselves.

This was discovered during a game of trading tokens with a human for a nut to eat—the parrots went a step beyond, giving a token to a neighbor that did not have one, even if the neighbor was not their friend.

Unfortunately, because they live for so long and can form strong emotional bonds with their human owners (as well as being beautiful, interesting, and entertaining pets with the ability to say many words), they are considered to be valuable for the pet industry. Every year, around 20% of the wild population is captured for the pet trade and more than half of these birds die before they ever reach their sellers. This is just one example of how humans aren't always smart!

Orca

Measuring around 26 ft (8 meters) long, weighing a staggering 12,000 lbs (5400 kg) and living for up to 90 years, Orcas are incredible, beautiful creatures. Orcas typically swim around 100 miles (160 km) per day, so keeping them in swimming pools in theme parks must be hugely frustrating for them.

Did you know:

Orcas are sometimes called "Killer Whales," but there are thousands of predators in the world that aren't given that nickname! There are no records of a wild orca killing a human.

They have one of the largest brains of all ocean mammals, weighing as much as 15 lbs (6.8 kg). Scientists have found they are amazingly well-wired for sensing and analyzing their immense, watery, three-dimensional environment. They've discovered this by scanning a dead Orca's brain.

It is thought that Orcas have well developed language and their vocabulary varies from place to place (with local dialects, just like in the human world). They teach one another methods of hunting as well as other behaviors that can last for many generations. This sort of social memory is a sure sign of intelligent survivors!

In the Arctic, orcas have been seen following and listening out for the sounds of fishing boats to eat the fish (such as herring) that spill out of the bulging nets. These coordinated hunters are one of the most successful predators on the planet, and don't always rely on fishing nets full of food.

As well as their intelligence that leads them to food, orcas have been observed showing emotional intelligence. A female orca called Tahlequah gave birth and her calf died soon after. She carried her dead baby for 17 days and covered 990 miles (1600 km) whilst carrying it in a demonstration of grief and sorrow.

Portia Spider

There are around 40,000 **species** of spider in the world. These arachnids are incredibly well suited to their environments and live on every continent except for Antarctica. Almost all spiders have venom for killing their prey and produce silk that they use as a building material, and as a way of getting around.

There are some spiders that make loose, flat webs, some that build dense, three-dimensional web funnels in corners, or underground lairs with trapdoors, and even underwater bubble-shaped webs. Some spiders don't make webs at all but go out hunting for food, catching what they can, like flies and other insects . . . even birds!

The portia spider (*Portia fimbriata*) not only has excellent eyesight (better than that of a cat), it can jump very quickly and accurately 50 times its 0.4 in (10 mm) body length and is a skillful and clever hunter that eats other (sometimes much larger) spiders!

Ethologists have observed that when it gets close to the web of another spider (of a different **species**), it stands on the edge of the web and plucks the strands (with its legs and palps) to make a series of vibrations—119 different vibration patterns have been observed! This mimics the vibrations that a struggling fly would make. This entices the other spider to come closer to investigate before being stunned and eaten.

This use of trial and error, aggressive mimicry, and deception make the portia spider a really smart and truly remarkable animal!

Dog

To many of us, seeing dogs is a part of everyday life as they are a popular choice of household pet. This is due to their beauty, loyalty, and personality as well as their companionship and affection.

During the 16,000 years since dogs were first **domesticated** from wild wolves by our ancestors (some scientists think this may have happened 30,000 years ago), they have had other important roles too—as protectors and hunters, helping us to herd our flocks, and even keeping us warm at night!

Because of their amazing sense of smell (up to 10,000 times better than ours), they are also used to sniff out illegal drugs, explosives, and other chemicals—some can even smell when people have particular diseases! Some breeds of dogs (there are around 500 worldwide) can be trained to act as the "eyes" of blind people—allowing them live more independently.

Australian wild dogs called Dingoes (*Canis dingo*) eat mammals, reptiles, birds, insects, crabs, fish, frogs, seeds, and grains. Just like their distant cousins, the wolves, when their prey is just too big and quick for them to tackle alone (like kangaroos that can punch and kick) they hunt in packs of up to 15 individuals. They can surround their prey whilst communicating with each other about what to do next, through a series of howls, growls, chortles, yelps, whines, chatters, snorts, and purrs. Dingoes very rarely bark like our pet dogs.

Did you know:

Some scientists suggest that dogs' friendly nature as reliable companions and pets is a sign that they have been manipulating us for thousands of years . . . and will probably continue for thousands of years to come!

The instinct of some dogs to chase their prey has been used by shepherds and farmers for thousands of years. Dogs are trained to gently and skillfully scare very large herds of cows, sheep, and other animals from one place to another—often from a huge pasture or ranch into much smaller enclosures. This can even be a sport! It shows off both the skill of the handler and the sheep dog, with complex routes for the dog to persuade the animals to take before arriving in a pen.

Chimpanzee

One of our closest related **species**, these forest dwelling apes are truly remarkable. We know this because they've been observed for decades in the wild, zoos, animal parks, and even as household pets. British primatologist, Jane Goodall has pioneered much of this research in Tanzania since 1960.

In the worlds of animal behavior and animal intelligence, their use of objects around them as tools is legendary. This includes using plant stems, twigs, branches, leaves, and rocks—in many different ways . . .

Drinking
using chewed up leaves as sponges to soak up plant sap

Feeding
cracking nuts open with rocks and "fishing" for termites, honey, and ants using twigs

Cleaning
using leaves as body wipes after eating sticky fruits

Exploring
investigating out-of-reach objects

Healing
eating hairy leaves which help to flush out worms in their intestines

Fighting
waving branches and throwing stones and rocks as missiles

In the wild, after bushfires, chimpanzees have been seen to understand the basics of fire, being able to predict its direction of travel. In captivity, a well-trained Bonobo (*Pan paniscus*, a chimpanzee sibling) have even been seen to build a fire and cook a marshmallow on the fire, before extinguishing it with water!

Such is their ability to learn, a Bonobo has also been observed playing the computer game Pac Man. Obviously this happened in a laboratory, not in the wild or randomly at an amusement arcade, but he mastered the game and understood that he had to avoid the ghosts unless he had "eaten" a power pellet.

Back in 1961, a chimpanzee named Ham was one of the first chimps to travel into space when he made a 16.5 minute journey 157 m (253 km) from Earth at a speed of 5857 mp/h (9426 km/h). During this flight, (which included six minutes of weightlessness), he would have had to pull levers and press buttons in the correct order. The results of this experiment paved the way for the USA's first human astronaut (Alan Shephard) later that year. Ham returned and lived for another 22 years, probably quite happy to be on the ground! Many animals sent into space sadly never returned, but have helped us to understand and improve our technology and our knowledge of space, our own planet, and animal intelligence.

A famous chimpanzee called Washoe was taught American Sign Language (invented for deaf people to communicate with each other). She learned over 100 different signs which made it possible for her to "talk" to her human housemates and even teach her own baby some words. She loved looking at books, shoes, brushing her teeth, and painting pictures.

Cat

There are around 70 different cat breeds in the world, and just like dogs, these vary by their size, color, hair length, and other physical features. They are one of the most popular choices of house pet in the world because they are soft, cuddly, and have their own personalities. Different cat breeds also vary in intelligence!

Scientifically, cats are quite difficult to persuade to participate in research, which is actually evidence of intelligence! Cats have 300 million **neurons** in their brains (compared to a dog, which has 160 million), so we know they are wired for intelligence. Their brains only weigh around 1 oz (30 g), but they have a similar shape and structure to a human brain (highly folded which increases the overall surface area of it), and this is thought to help with their intelligence.

When scientists have managed to get cats to take part in their experiments, they've seen that cats can follow the gaze of an unfamiliar human looking from one place to another, and then toward a food reward.

From a very young age, cats play with each other. A lot of this includes play fighting, which is not only family bonding time, but also preparation for the real world. This is also seen throughout the larger cat world—in lions, cheetahs, tigers etc. They all need to how to quietly find and hunt for food, and kill it quickly. The cuddly house cat no longer needs to do this, but given the chance many will still go wild and catch mice, rats, and wild garden birds—sometimes without even eating them.

Cats certainly have great memories—a good example of this is when a cat owner packs their suitcase and the cat starts sulking because it can clearly remember the last time they went away and left the cat alone without daily affection.

Some cats might scratch at an outside door that they've never been through, but have seen you go through. This seems obvious to us, but it's a sign that they have learned and remembered the purpose of that door.

Cats can sometimes predict where and when a moving object will reappear (like a ball rolling behind a book) as well as understanding that just because it can't see an object that was visible a moment ago, the object still exists, but has just been hidden. This is known as **"object permanence,"** something human babies learn at around 9 months old.

Orangutan

In the forests of South-East Asia, the great apes called Orangutans (which translates as "Man of the Forest") spend quite a lot of their time alone or in very small family groups, avoiding predators while exploring the looking for food. They eat fruits, seeds, leaves, tree bark, eggs, fungi, and honey—some of which are quite hard to find.

In captivity, they have a very different life, often living with many more orangutans than they would in the wild, with no predators, and having a much easier time finding food.

Because of this, they have been seen to have changed their behavior, most amazingly (in a zoo in Switzerland) developing a new language of gestures and facial expressions! Around seven signals like this were developed, mostly inviting another orangutan to come and play or to get food. This shows that they have the ability to learn new languages.

In another study, an orangutan called Rocky has learned how to mimic (copy) the tone and pitch of human speech which is another jigsaw piece in understanding how human speech first evolved.

There are a few examples of orangutans having non-orangutan friends that they really love and care for. At a wildlife sanctuary in America, an orangutan called Suriya met a stray dog which he instantly befriended. He and Roscoe (named by his human friends) spend all their time together playing, swimming, and cuddling.

In a Swedish zoo, Naong the orangutan was put into a study alongside humans to see if they could predict what different drinks would taste like if mixed together. He was offered cherry, rhubarb, and lemon juice as well as apple cider vinegar, each color-coded. After learning the four flavors he was able to predict which combinations of the drinks would (or wouldn't) taste good. This is known as "affective forecasting," and shows advanced mental capacities which must be useful in the wild.

Pigeon

There are around 351 **species** of pigeons in the world, all in the Columbidae Family (alongside doves).

5000 years ago in Ancient Egypt, the amazing navigation skills of homing pigeons were being used to deliver messages over huge distances. They were also used during World War I and II to send messages to soldiers behind enemy lines (sometimes as far as 240 m/390 km away). Sometimes, when they landed and returned to their coop, a buzzer or bell would sound—like a modern day email or phone notification! They've also been used to deliver letters, medicines, and smuggle things like cell phones and SIM cards into prisons.

Did you know:

Homing pigeons not only have great homing instincts, but in laboratory experiments, they've been shown to be able to recognize the difference between paintings by the artists Van Gogh and Mark Chagall!

A 20th Century American psychologist called Burrhus Frederic Skinner invented a device called a "Skinner Box" (which was a bit like a vending machine) where a disc is pressed to dispense food. Pigeons proved to be really good at using these and learned that they would only receive food when a green disc was pressed, but they got nothing when the disc was blue. They were then shown different color photographs one at a time and slowly worked out that they could only get food by pressing the disc when a picture had trees in it. Another set of images showed water in different forms and they became trained to only peck when they saw a lake, a raindrop, or snow.

The researchers then tried the experiment with four different human faces and different expressions (happy, angry, surprised, and disgusted)—only getting food when a certain face or expression was shown. They passed this one too, showing that pigeons can learn ideas as well as being able to tell the difference between various shapes and objects.

Skinner and his performing pigeons were so successful that during WWII the US Navy took his idea of a pigeon-controlled missile very seriously. Three pigeons who'd been trained to recognize the target (battleships) would be inside a missile hurtling towards the target with a window for them to look at it. If they pecked at the center of an image, the missile would fly straight, but if they pecked to the side, the missile would go off course. The project didn't go ahead in the end as it was thought to be too dangerous!

Drongo Bird

In the Kalahari Desert in Southern Africa, the fork-tailed drongo (Dicrurus adsimilis) is a smart trickster indeed.

It shares the desert with many other animals including meerkats (*Suricata suricatta*) who dig in the sand for insects and other small animals to eat. One of the meerkats' enemies are eagles who fly far above, scanning the desert for food.

When the Drongo Bird sees an eagle, it makes a quick noise that alerts the meerkats of the danger and they all run and hide in their burrows. Once they surface and resume their digging for grubs and bugs, the drongo does it again—even if there is no danger coming. Once they're safely underground, it swoops down to the ground and steals their food!

Later, it might try this again, but once the meerkats know it is a trick, they ignore it. A little later on, the drongo will imitate the alarm sound usually made by the meerkat scout (the meerkat who look, smell and listen out for danger).

.Thinking it's their scout making the sound and danger is close, they all head underground once more, only to surface and find that the drongo has stolen their food again!

Fork-tailed drongos are thought to be able to make up to 51 different calls to trick other animals—they actually get almost a quarter of all of their food in this way. Scientists think that drongos have something called "Theory of Mind," which means they can understand the minds of others—something usually only seen in humans. In Australia, drongo is a slang term for an idiot, but these birds are far from that! Their use of timing, mimicry, and gaining trust is truly remarkable animal behavior and gives this bird a place in the smart animal hall of fame (and this book)!

Glossary

Anesthetic
A substance that causes a loss of feeling or awareness, like when you go to the dentist.

Biomimicry
When people use ideas from nature to come up with solutions to problems.

Cognitive abilities
How much a being is able to think and reason.

Colony
A group of people or creatures that build a home in another area.

Dextrous
Skillful, quick cleverness.

Domesticating
The process of working with wild animals to make them safe around humans (either as pets or as working animals).

Ethology
The science of animal behavior.

Ethologist
Someone who studies animal behavior.

Evolution
The process by which species adapt and change over time in relation to their environment.

Homo sapiens
The name of the species to which human beings belong.

Invertebrate
Animals without a backbone or a bony skeleton.

Naturalized
An animal or plant that is not native to an area, but has been introduced by humans (accidentally or on purpose) and has adapted to the area and grown its population.

Object permanence
The capacity to understand that an object that was visible just a moment ago and now has escaped our field of view still exists.

Omnivrous
An animal that can survive on both plants and animal matter (meat).

Opposable (thumbs)

When the thumb is attached to a different part of the hand than the fingers, allowing it to be used to grip and manipulate objects. Humans and some other animals like gorillas and chimpanzees have opposable thumbs.

Neurons

The cells that make up an animal's nervous system. They transport information in a similar way to networking cables, which connect computers.

Primitive

Something in an early or simple stage of development.

Species

The smallest classification for group of animals or plants— a group of organisms that is unique to themselves.

Symbiosis/Symbiotic

Two different organisms form a very close relationship from which they both benefit.

Vertebrate

An animal with a backbone and a bony skeleton.

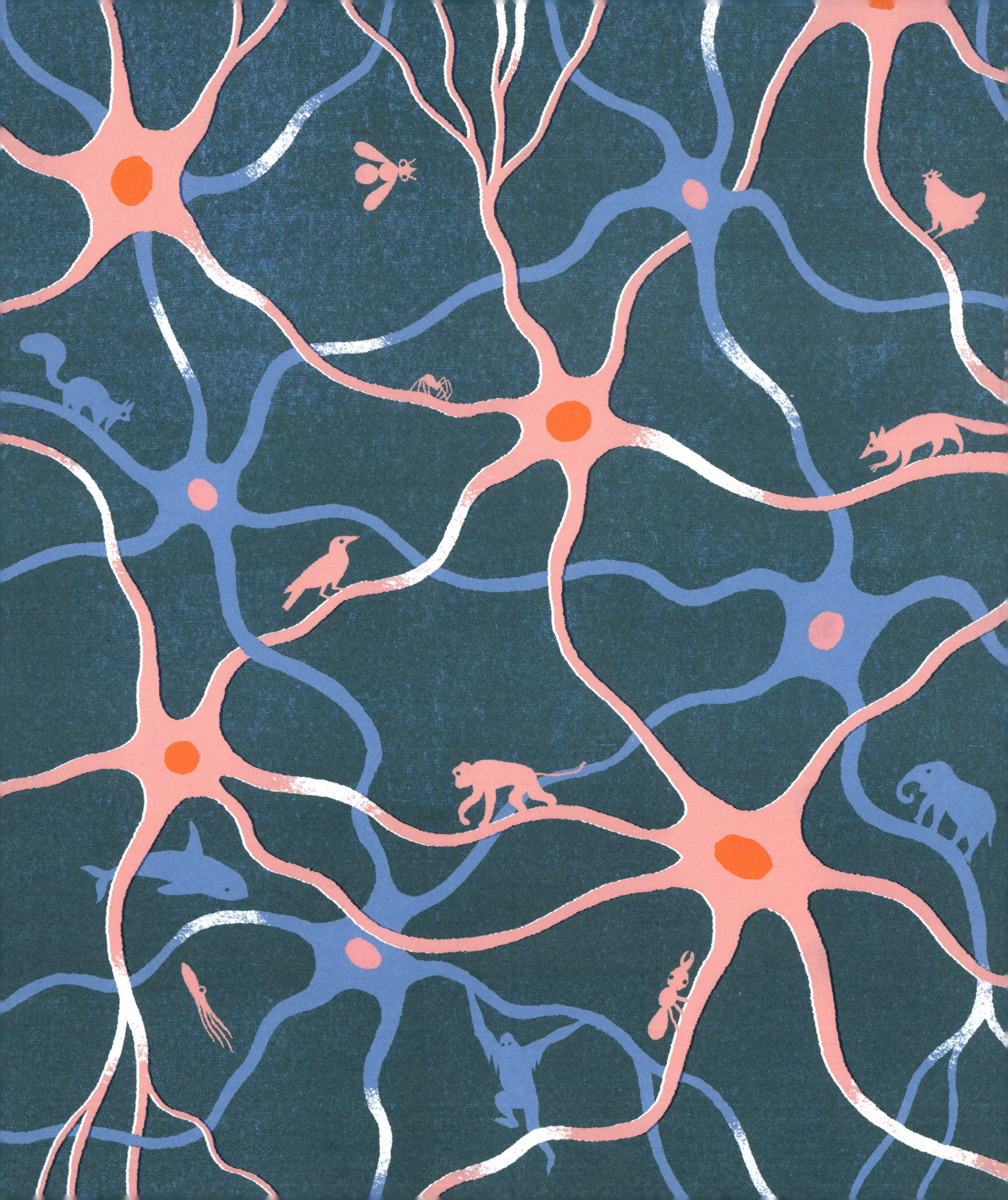